FOOD LOVERS

ITALIAN

FOOD LOVERS

ITALIAN

RECIPES SELECTED BY MARIKA KUCEROVA

Trans
Atlantic
Press

All recipes serve four people, unless otherwise indicated.

CONTENTS

ANTIPASTO OF MIXED VEGETABLES

Ingredients

2 zucchinis (courgettes)

2 eggplants (aubergines)

2 red bell peppers

2 white onions

2 tomatoes

2 garlic cloves

6 tbsp olive oil

1 sprig rosemary, chopped

Lemon wedges, for garnishing

Salt and freshly ground pepper

Method

Prep and cook time: 30 min plus 40 min standing time

1 Rinse the zucchinis (courgettes) and eggplants (aubergines). Remove the tops and stems. Slice lengthwise into ½ cm / ¼ inch thick slices.

2 Salt the eggplant slices and let stand for 30 minutes. Soak them in water for about 10 minutes to remove the salt.

3 Slice the bell peppers in half. Remove the ribs and seeds. Slice in half again.

4 Peel the onions and slice into wedges.

5 Rinse the tomatoes and cut out the stems. Slice in half.

6 Peel and finely chop the garlic and combine with the olive oil.

7 Pat the eggplant slices dry. Brush all the vegetables with oil.

8 Heat a ridged skillet or griddle pan and cook the vegetables in batches, turning frequently and brushing occasionally with the oil, until they are tender.

9 Arrange the vegetables on a platter. Remove the skin from the peppers if desired. Season with salt and pepper. Sprinkle with the rosemary and garnish with lemon wedges.

MUSSELS AU GRATIN

Ingredients

1 kg / 2¼ lb fresh mussels

20 g / 1 cup fresh parsley

8 tbsp olive oil

200 g / 2 cups bread crumbs

½ red chili, deseeded and chopped

1 tbsp freshly grated Parmesan cheese

1 garlic clove, chopped

Salt and freshly ground pepper

Method

Prep and cook time: 25 min

1 Preheat the oven to 200C (400F / Gas Mark 6).

2 Scrub the mussels well with a small metal brush and wash under running water. Put into a large pan and cover with water, put a lid on the pan and bring to a boil over a high heat.

3 Cook until the mussels open (throw away any that do not open). Drain (reserve 250 ml / 1 cup of the cooking water), then remove the empty halves of the shells and place the halves containing the mussels on a baking tray.

4 Wash the parsley, shake dry and chop finely. Heat 3 tbsp olive oil in a frying pan and fry the bread crumbs, stirring, until golden brown.

5 Mix together the parsley, chili, bread crumbs, Parmesan cheese, garlic, the remaining oil and 1–2 tbsp of the mussel water. Season with salt and pepper.

6 Place a little of the mixture on top of each mussel and press down slightly. Put the baking tray into the preheated oven for about 2–3 minutes, until the gratin topping is nicely browned.

BRUSCHETTA WITH TOMATOES AND BASIL

Ingredients

2 garlic cloves

3 beef tomatoes

2 basil sprigs

1 tbsp lemon juice,

8 thin slices baguette

2–3 tbsp olive oil

Salt and freshly ground pepper

Method

Prep and cook time: 20 min

1 Preheat the oven to 240C (475F / Gas Mark 9).

2 Peel the garlic. Slice the cloves in half.

3 Quarter the tomatoes. Remove the seeds and chop.

4 Remove the basil leaves from the stem. Set a few aside for garnishing. Coarsely chop the rest.

5 Mix the basil leaves with the tomatoes and lemon juice. Season with salt and pepper to taste.

6 Toast the bread slices in the oven (lay directly on a rack) for about 2 minutes, until golden brown.

7 Rub the hot slices with the garlic and drizzle with olive oil. Place some tomatoes on top of each slice. Garnish with the reserved basil leaves and serve.

ASPARAGUS IN PROSCIUTTO

Ingredients

32 asparagus spears (about 900 g / 2 lb)

16 slices prosciutto

4 tbsp freshly grated Parmesan cheese

5 tbsp olive oil

2 handfuls arugula (rocket)

3 tbsp white wine vinegar

Salt and freshly ground pepper

Method
Prep and cook time: 35 min

1 Preheat the oven to 200C (400F / Gas Mark 6).

2 Peel the lower third of the asparagus spears and place in boiling, salted water. Simmer gently for about 2–3 minutes, then drain, refresh in cold water and drain thoroughly.

3 Wrap each slice of prosciutto around 2 asparagus spears and lay side by side in an ovenproof baking dish. Sprinkle with a little freshly ground pepper.

4 Mix the Parmesan cheese with 3 tbsp olive oil and scatter over the asparagus. Bake in the oven for 6–8 minutes.

5 Wash the arugula (rocket), remove any hard stalks and arrange on plates. Drizzle with 2 tbsp olive oil and the vinegar. Sprinkle with salt and pepper and lay the asparagus on top. Serve immediately.

MINESTRONE SOUP

Ingredients

4 tomatoes

Olive oil

2 onions, finely chopped

2 carrots, finely diced

2 small zucchini (courgettes), finely diced

2 garlic cloves, peeled and crushed

250 g / 2 cups passata (sieved tomatoes)

750 ml / 2½ cups vegetable broth (stock)

600 g / 3 cups canned butter beans

Basil leaves, chopped

Freshly grated Parmesan cheese

Salt and freshly ground pepper

Wholewheat bread, to serve

Method

Prep and cook time: 35 min

1 Drop the tomatoes into boiling water for a few seconds, then skin, halve, deseed and finely dice.

2 Heat 2 tbsp oil in a pan and sweat the onions, carrots, zucchini (courgettes) and garlic over a low heat for 2–3 minutes, stirring.

3 Add the passata. Cook over a very low heat until reduced slightly, then add the broth (stock).

4 Bring to a boil, stir in the diced tomato and simmer over a low heat for about 10 minutes.

5 Stir in the drained beans and basil leaves and cook gently for a further 1 minute.

6 Season to taste with salt and pepper. Sprinkle with Parmesan cheese and serve with hearty wholewheat bread.

BREAD SALAD WITH TOMATOES

Ingredients

1 ciabatta loaf, day old

8 tbsp olive oil

8 tomatoes

20 g / 1 cup fresh basil leaves

50 g / ½ cup black olives, pitted

2 red onions

1 garlic clove

½ cucumber

2 tbsp white balsamic vinegar

2 tbsp lemon juice

Salt and freshly ground pepper

Method

Prep and cook time: 30 min

1 Cut the ciabatta into cubes. Sauté in 3 tbsp of olive oil until golden brown and crispy. Drain the croutons on paper towel.

2 Rinse the tomatoes, remove the stalks and slice into wedges.

3 Remove the basil leaves from the stems. Coarsely chop.

4 Slice the olives in half.

5 Peel the onion and cut in half. Slice into strips.

6 Peel and finely chop the garlic.

7 Peel the cucumber and cut in half lengthwise. Remove the seeds and slice.

8 Put the tomatoes, olives, onion, cucumber and garlic in a dish. Mix with the remaining oil, balsamic vinegar and lemon juice. Season to taste with salt and pepper. Allow to marinate for 10 minutes.

9 Mix in the basil and croutons. Season to taste again and serve.

CROSTINI WITH BEAN SPREAD

Ingredients

450 g / 2 cups canned butter beans, drained

2 garlic cloves, crushed

2–3 tbsp olive oil

Baguette or ciabatta

1 tbsp fresh thyme, chopped

100 g / 1 cup black olives, to serve

100 g / 1 cup green olives, to serve

Salt and freshly ground pepper

Method

Prep and cook time: 15 min

1 Drain the beans and rinse well.

2 Purée the beans with the garlic and enough oil to make a thick paste. Season with salt.

3 Spread on toasted slices of baguette or ciabatta. Season with thyme and freshly ground pepper and serve with olives.

HAM RISOTTO WITH GREEN ASPARAGUS

Ingredients

900 g / 2 lb green asparagus

4 tbsp olive oil

2 garlic cloves, chopped

1 liter / 4 cups vegetable broth (stock)

300 g / 1½ cups risotto rice

150 g / 6 oz cooked ham

2 tbsp butter, flaked

50 g / ½ cup freshly grated
Parmesan cheese

Salt and freshly ground pepper

Parsley leaves, for garnishing

Method

Prep and cook time: 40 min

1 Peel the lower third of the asparagus stalks. Trim the ends and slice into bite-size pieces.

2 Heat 3 tbsp of oil in a pan. Add the garlic and sauté briefly. Add the asparagus and sauté briefly. Add a little water and continue cooking for 4–5 minutes. Cover and set aside.

3 Bring the broth (stock) to a simmer in a small pan.

4 Sauté the rice in the remaining oil in a large pan. Gradually add the hot broth, stirring occasionally, over the next 20 minutes (only add more broth as it evaporates / the rice absorbs it) until al dente.

5 Finely chop the ham.

6 Five minutes before the rice is done, add the asparagus and warm through.

7 Stir the ham, flaked butter and grated Parmesan into the rice. Season to taste with salt and pepper. Garnish with the parsley.

SPAGHETTI ALLA PUTTANESCA

Ingredients

100 g / 1 cup black olives, pitted

6 anchovy fillets

4 garlic cloves

2 dried chili peppers

3 tbsp olive oil

400 g / 2 cups canned tomatoes, chopped

450 g / 1 lb spaghetti

1 tbsp capers

Salt and freshly ground pepper

Method
Prep and cook time: 25 min

1 Coarsely chop the olives and the anchovies.

2 Peel and finely chop the garlic. Sauté in hot oil for about 2 minutes with the chili peppers and the anchovies.

3 Add the tomatoes and simmer gently for about 10 minutes.

4 Cook the spaghetti in well-salted boiling water until al dente.

5 Add the capers and olives to the sauce. Season with salt and pepper.

6 Combine the sauce with the well-drained spaghetti. Serve.

PIZZA MARGHERITA

Ingredients

For the base:

1½ tsp easy-bake yeast

¼ tsp sugar

450 g / 1 lb all-purpose (plain) flour

2 tbsp olive oil

1 tsp salt

For the topping:

4 tbsp olive oil, plus extra for drizzling

1 garlic clove, chopped

1 shallot, chopped

400 g / 2 cups canned tomatoes, chopped

2 tbsp tomato paste (purée)

1 tsp dried oregano

400 g / 2 cups mozzarella cheese

2 fresh tomatoes, sliced

2 tsp fresh oregano leaves

24 black olives

Salt and freshly ground pepper

Method

Prep and cook time: 45 min, plus I h resting time

1 Mix the yeast in a bowl with about $^1/_3$ cup lukewarm water and the sugar.

2 Add the flour, olive oil and salt and knead to a pliable dough, adding a little water if the dough is too dry. Cover and put to rise in a warm place for about 1 hour.

3 Preheat the oven to 220C (425F / Gas Mark 7).

4 Heat the oil in a pan and sauté the garlic and shallot until translucent.

5 Add the canned tomatoes and tomato paste (purée) and stew gently for about 20 minutes. Season with oregano, salt and pepper.

6 Divide the dough into 4 and roll out on a lightly floured surface into circles of approximately 22 cm / 9 inch diameter, leaving the edges a little thicker.

7 Put the pizza bases on 2 greased cookie sheets and spread with the tomato sauce. Slice the mozzarella thinly and lay on the pizzas. Drizzle with a little olive oil.

8 Bake in the preheated oven for about 20 minutes. Take out and top with fresh tomato slices, oregano and olives.

RED MULLET
WITH BEANS AND TOMATOES

Ingredients

450 g / 1 lb fava (broad) beans

Handful of basil leaves

3 tomatoes

8 red mullet fillets, with skin

2 tbsp butter

1 garlic clove

3 tbsp olive oil

5 tbsp fish broth (stock)

Cayenne pepper

2 tsp white wine vinegar

Salt and freshly ground pepper

Method
Prep and cook time: 25 min

1 Remove the beans from the pods and cook in boiling water for 10 minutes. Refresh in cold water and slip the beans out of their skins.

2 Rinse the basil and shake dry. Remove the leaves from the stems and slice into strips, reserving a few whole leaves to garnish.

3 Blanch the tomatoes for a few seconds. Immerse in cold water. Remove the skins, quarter and deseed. Chop and season lightly with salt and pepper.

4 Rinse the fish fillets under cold water and pat dry.

5 Heat 1 tbsp butter in a large skillet. Fry the fillets for about 4 minutes each side. Arrange on 4 warmed plates, skin side up.

6 Swirl the chopped tomatoes around the skillet with the remaining butter. Add the beans, fish broth (stock) and basil strips. Combine well and pour over the fillets.

7 Peel and crush the garlic. Mix with the oil, cayenne pepper and vinegar and season to taste. Drizzle over the fish fillets.

8 Garnish with the reserved basil leaves and serve lukewarm.

PENNE WITH CHICKEN, PEA AND LEMON SAUCE

PRAWNS

Ingredients

1 shallot

1 garlic clove

2 chicken breasts

2 tbsp butter

1 tbsp flour

150 ml / 2/3 cup chicken broth (stock)

80 ml / 1/3 cup ~~whipping cream~~ creme fraise

150 g / 1 cup frozen peas, thawed

1 lemon

450 g / 1 lb penne

1 tbsp finely chopped parsley

Salt and freshly ground pepper

1/4 cup parmesan chz

Method

Prep and cook time: 30 min

1 Peel and finely chop the shallot and garlic.

2 Slice the chicken breasts into thin strips.

3 Sauté the chicken, shallot and garlic in hot butter. Sprinkle the flour on top. Mix and sauté briefly.

4 Add the broth (stock) and cream while stirring. Season with salt and pepper and bring to a boil. Add the peas and simmer over low heat for about 10 minutes. Stir occasionally.

5 Zest the lemon and squeeze out the juice.

6 Cook the penne in well-salted boiling water until al dente.

7 Add the parsley and lemon zest to the cream sauce. Season with a little lemon juice, salt and pepper.

8 Divide the well-drained pasta among the plates. Pour the sauce over the top and serve.

SEA BASS WITH GREMOLATA

Ingredients

1 lemon

½ bunch flat-leaf parsley

2 garlic cloves

8 small sea bass fillets

2–3 tbsp butter

2 handfuls arugula (rocket)

4 tsp white balsamic vinegar

Method

Prep and cook time: 20 min

1 Finely grate the lemon peel. Chop the parsley. Peel the garlic and dice very finely. Combine the three to make the gremolata.

2 Squeeze the lemon and turn the fish fillets in the juice. Fry the fish in butter on both sides.

3 Put the gremolata on top of the fish, put a lid on the pan and leave to stand over a low heat for 2 minutes.

4 Wash and sort the arugula (rocket) and shake dry. Put a little onto each of 4 warmed plates and sprinkle with balsamic vinegar. Add a couple of fish fillets to each plate and serve immediately.

VEAL AND MOZZARELLA PARCELS

Ingredients

For the parcels:

8 thin veal cutlets

4 slices prosciutto

150 g / 1½ cups mozzarella cheese

2 garlic cloves

1 tsp chopped fresh rosemary

1 tsp chopped fresh thyme

16 sage leaves

2 tbsp olive oil

2 tbsp butter

Salt and freshly ground pepper

Method

Prep and cook time: 25 min

1 Put the veal cutlets between two pieces of plastic wrap (clingfilm) and pound lightly so they are very thin and all the same thickness. Season with salt and pepper.

2 Cut the prosciutto slices in half. Thinly slice the mozzarella. Peel and finely chop the garlic.

3 Divide the prosciutto, mozzarella, garlic and herbs among the cutlets. Season with salt and pepper.

4 Roll up the cutlets, securing with tooth picks (cocktail sticks), to make parcels.

5 Heat the oil and butter in a large skillet and sauté the parcels, turning occasionally, for about 5 minutes, until they turn brown and the cheese begins to melt.

6 Arrange the parcels on a platter and serve.

SPAGHETTI WITH CLAMS AND SQUID

Ingredients

400 g / 1 lb small squid, cleaned and ready to cook

400 g / 1 lb clams

1 lemon

2 cloves garlic

100 ml / 7 tbsp white wine

400 g / 1 lb spaghetti

1 leek

4 tbsp olive oil

4 tsp white vermouth

Method

Prep and cook time: 35 min

1 Rinse, drain and coarsely chop the squid. Discard any clams that are open.

2 Rinse the lemon under hot water. Remove the zest and squeeze out the juice.

3 Peel the garlic and slice.

4 Bring the wine, half of the lemon juice and 100 ml / ½ cup of water to boil in a pan. Put the clams in the pan and cover. Simmer for about 8 minutes or until the clams open. Discard any unopened clams.

5 Cook the spaghetti according to the package instructions.

6 Remove the roots and trim the ragged ends of the leek. Slice the white and bright green parts on a diagonal into rings.

7 Sauté the squid in 4 tbsp of oil for about 2 minutes. Add the leek and the sliced garlic. Continue to sauté for another 2–3 minutes.

8 Pour in the vermouth and the remainder of the lemon juice. Simmer briefly.

9 Toss everything together with the well drained spaghetti (and a little of the pasta water). Season with salt and pepper.

BAKED POLENTA GNOCCHI

Ingredients

250 g / 1¼ cups quick-cooking polenta

For the sauce:

4 tbsp olive oil

1 onion, chopped

1 garlic clove, chopped

450 g / 1 lb ripe tomatoes

1 tbsp basil, shredded

70 g / ⅓ cup butter

50 g / ½ cup freshly grated Parmesan cheese

Salt and freshly ground pepper

Method

Prep and cook time: 50 min

1 Prepare the polenta according to the package instructions.

2 Heat the olive oil and sweat the onion and garlic until soft.

3 Blanch the tomatoes briefly, refresh in cold water, then skin, quarter, deseed and dice finely.

4 Add to the onion with salt and pepper and simmer for 2–3 minutes. Stir in the basil.

5 Preheat the oven to 200C (400F / Gas Mark 6).

6 Butter an ovenproof dish.

7 Using a moistened tablespoon, cut gnocchi out of the polenta and arrange in the dish.

8 Pour the tomato sauce over, sprinkle with grated Parmesan cheese and dot with the remaining butter.

9 Bake in the preheated oven for 25–30 minutes.

BAKED COD
WITH POTATOES, OLIVES AND TOMATOES

Ingredients

675 g / 1½ lb new potatoes

1 onion, chopped

150 ml / ²/₃ cup vegetable broth (stock)

675 g / 1½ lb cod fillets

450 g / 1 lb cherry tomatoes

100 g / 1 cup black pitted olives

Juice of 1 lemon

2 tbsp olive oil

1 tbsp chopped fresh parsley leaves

Salt and freshly ground pepper

Method
Prep and cook time: 45 min

1 Preheat the oven to 180C (350F / Gas Mark 4).

2 Thoroughly wash and slice the potatoes. Place in a heat-resistant baking dish with the chopped onion.

3 Pour the vegetable broth (stock) over the top. Season with salt and pepper. Bake in the oven for about 15 minutes.

4 Rinse the cod fillets, pat dry and cut into large pieces.

5 Remove the dish from the oven, add the tomatoes, fish and olives and season with salt and pepper. Drizzle with the lemon juice and olive oil.

6 Continue cooking for another 15 minutes (add a little water if necessary). Garnish with parsley and serve.

SPINACH CANNELLONI

Ingredients

Olive oil, for greasing

250 g / 9 oz cannelloni tubes
(no pre-cook type)

For the filling:

500 g / 6 cups spinach

200 g / 2 cups ricotta cheese

1 egg

Nutmeg

Salt and freshly ground pepper

For the tomatoes:

225 g / ½ lb tomatoes

1 shallot

1 garlic clove

1 tbsp olive oil

For the béchamel sauce:

1 tbsp butter

1 tbsp flour

250 ml / 1 cup milk

75 g / ¾ cup freshly grated
Parmesan cheese

Salt and freshly ground pepper

Method

Prep and cook time: 1 h

1 Lightly grease an ovenproof dish with a little olive oil. Preheat the oven to 200C (400F / Gas Mark 6).

2 Wash the spinach well, put into a pan dripping wet and heat over a medium heat until it wilts. Drain, refresh in cold water, drain again and squeeze out excess water.

3 Roughly chop the spinach and mix with the mashed ricotta. Stir in the egg and season with salt, pepper and nutmeg.

4 Spoon the mixture into the cannelloni tubes and place them side by side in the baking dish.

5 Drop the tomatoes into boiling water for a few seconds, refresh in cold water, then skin, quarter, deseed and chop roughly.

6 Peel and finely chop the shallot and garlic. Heat the oil and sauté the shallot and garlic then add the tomatoes and cook over a medium heat for about 5 minutes.

7 For the béchamel sauce, melt the butter, stir in the flour and cook for a couple of minutes without browning. Then gradually stir in the milk. Simmer for 10 minutes, season with salt and pepper and stir in half of the Parmesan.

8 Spread the tomatoes on the cannelloni. Pour the sauce over and sprinkle with the rest of the Parmesan cheese. Dot with butter and bake for about 30 minutes.

MARINATED VEGETABLES WITH SAUSAGE

Ingredients

12 small artichokes

1 lemon

2 garlic cloves

225 g / ½ lb salsiccia (fresh Italian sausage)

225 g / ½ lb mushrooms

4 red bell peppers

About 160 ml / ⅔ cup olive oil

3 sprigs rosemary

50 g / ½ cup green olives, pitted

50 g / ½ cup black olives, pitted

20 g / 1 tbsp capers

Freshly ground pepper

Method

Prep and cook time: 40 min
Marinating time: at least 2 h

1 Rinse, clean and remove the tips (the upper $1/3$) of the artichokes. Remove the tough outer leaves. Remove the stem, the lower portion of the hard bottom and any fibers.

2 Squeeze the juice from the lemon. Pour some lemon juice over the artichokes (this prevents them from darkening).

3 Boil the artichokes in salted water for 8 minutes. Drain and allow to cool until lukewarm.

4 Peel the garlic cloves.

5 Cut the salsiccia into slices.

6 Clean the mushrooms. Slice any large ones in half.

7 Slice the bell peppers in half. Remove the ribs and seeds. Slice into wide strips.

8 Sauté the sausage pieces in 2 tbsp of hot oil. Put them in a flat dish.

9 Add the remaining lemon juice, garlic cloves, mushrooms, artichokes, peppers, rosemary, olives, capers and remaining olive oil. Season with pepper and mix together thoroughly. Allow to sit for at least 2 hours before serving.

PORK CUTLETS WITH TOMATOES, PESTO AND MOZZARELLA

Ingredients

2 large tomatoes

1 tbsp pitted green olives

1 tbsp pitted black olives

300 g / 1½ cups mozzarella cheese

4 pork cutlets

5 tbsp olive oil

2 tbsp butter

4 tbsp basil pesto

Pepper

Basil leaves, for garnishing

Method

Prep and cook time: 45 min

1 Preheat the oven to 200C (400F / Gas Mark 6).

2 Slice the tomatoes and olives.

3 Drain and slice the mozzarella.

4 Put the cutlets between 2 pieces of plastic wrap and flatten slightly with a mallet or rolling pin.

5 Heat 1 tbsp oil and the butter in a large skillet and sear the cutlets quickly for 30 seconds each side.

6 Grease an ovenproof dish with the remaining olive oil.

7 Put the cutlets in the dish. Spread 1 tbsp of pesto on each of the cutlets, sprinkle the sliced olives on top and then add the mozzarella. Season with a little pepper.

8 Bake for 10–15 minutes. Garnish with the basil leaves and serve.

LEMON RISOTTO WITH HERBS AND PINE NUTS

Ingredients

About 1 liter / 4 cups chicken broth (stock)

1 onion, peeled and finely chopped

2 garlic cloves, peeled and finely chopped

3 tbsp olive oil

400 g / 2 cups risotto rice

250 ml / 1 cup dry white wine

1 lemon, juice and zest

1 tbsp chopped fresh parsley leaves

3 tbsp pine nuts

3 tbsp freshly grated Parmesan cheese

1 tbsp butter

Lemon halves, for garnishing

Salt and freshly ground pepper

Method

Prep and cook time: 30 min

1 Heat the broth (stock) in a pan.

2 Sauté the onion and garlic in a skillet with 3 tbsp of hot oil.

3 Add the rice and sauté briefly. Pour in the wine. Bring the ingredients to a boil quickly then add the lemon juice and zest and a little hot broth.

4 Cook the risotto over medium heat, stirring constantly and adding more broth gradually as it is absorbed, until the rice is creamy but still firm (about 20 minutes).

5 Mix the parsley, pine nuts, Parmesan cheese and butter into the risotto. Season to taste with salt and pepper. Garnish with the lemon halves and serve.

CHICKEN WITH CAPONATA

Ingredients

4 chicken legs

8 sage leaves

2 garlic cloves, chopped

2 red chili peppers, deseeded and chopped

4 tbsp olive oil

2 tbsp lemon juice

For the caponata:

1 medium eggplant (aubergine)

1 celery stalk

4 tomatoes

2 tbsp olive oil

1 yellow bell pepper, deseeded and sliced

1 onion, sliced

50 g / ½ cup pitted black olives

1 tbsp capers

White wine vinegar

Salt and freshly ground pepper.

Method

Prep and cook time: 1 h 10 min

1 Preheat the oven to 180C (350F / Gas Mark 4).

2 Take the chicken legs and separate the drumstick from the thigh at the joint. Put one sage leaf under the skin of each piece of chicken.

3 Mix together the garlic, chili pepper, olive oil and lemon juice. Rub into the chicken and put in a roasting pan.

4 Bake the chicken in the preheated oven for about 40 minutes until golden brown.

5 Coarsely chop the eggplant (aubergine).

6 Reserve the celery stalk leaves for garnish. Slice the rest.

7 Blanch the tomatoes, immerse in cold water and remove the skins. Slice into quarters and remove the seeds.

8 Sauté the eggplant in hot oil until lightly browned.

9 Add the bell pepper, onion and sliced celery. Season with salt and pepper. Cook, covered, for about 10 minutes stirring occasionally.

10 Add the tomatoes, olives and capers. Cook, uncovered, for about 4 minutes more. Season to taste with the vinegar, salt and pepper.

11 Divide the vegetables among the plates and arrange the chicken pieces on top. Garnish with the reserved celery leaves and serve.

GNOCCHI WITH HAM AND SAGE

Ingredients

775 g / 1¾ lb floury potatoes

50 g / ½ cup ricotta cheese

1 egg yolk

75 g / ¾ cup freshly grated
Parmesan cheese

About 50 g / ½ cup flour, plus extra
for kneading

Nutmeg, freshly grated

250 ml / 1 cup whipping cream

2 tbsp crème fraîche

2 slices prosciutto

Salt and freshly ground pepper

Sage leaves, for garnishing

Method
Prep and cook time: 50 min

1 For the gnocchi, boil the potatoes for about
30 minutes until they can be pierced easily with
a knife.

2 Remove the potatoes from the pan, peel and
mash well. Mix quickly with the ricotta, egg yolk,
50 g / ½ cup of Parmesan, the flour, salt, pepper
and nutmeg to form a dough, adding a little water if
necessary.

3 Sprinkle the dough with flour and roll into long
ropes. Cut into pieces of equal size, roll them gently
and allow to rest on a floured work surface until all
the gnocchi have been made.

4 Bring the cream, crème fraîche and remaining
Parmesan cheese to a boil in a pan. Season to taste
with salt and pepper.

5 Chop the prosciutto into small pieces.

6 Cook the gnocchi in salted boiling water for
10 minutes. Remove the gnocchi with a slotted
spoon and drain. Swirl them around in the hot
sauce. Divide among plates or bowls. Sprinkle with
the ham and pepper. Garnish with sage and serve.

THYME AND LEMON CHICKEN

Ingredients

1 chicken, about 1.2 kg / 2½ lb

10 sprigs thyme

3 tbsp olive oil

250 ml / 1 cup white wine

4 lemons

Salt and freshly ground pepper

Method

Prep and cook time: 1 h

1 Preheat the oven to 180C (350F / Gas Mark 4).

2 Rinse the chicken and dry well. Divide into eight pieces.

3 Strip the leaves from half of the thyme sprigs. Put the leaves between the chicken skin and the meat. Season with salt and pepper.

4 Heat the oil in a roasting pan and brown the chicken on all sides. Pour in the white wine.

5 Quarter the lemons and add them to the pan along with the remaining thyme sprigs.

6 Roast for about 30 minutes, or until the chicken is cooked through, basting occasionally.

TOMATO AND MOZZARELLA LASAGNA

Ingredients

Olive oil, for greasing

2 garlic cloves, finely chopped

400 g / 2 cups canned tomatoes, chopped

2 sprigs basil

350 g / ¾ lb mozzarella cheese

12 lasagna sheets, no-precook type

75 g / ¾ cup Parmesan cheese

Salt and freshly ground pepper

For the béchamel sauce:

50 g / ¼ cup butter

3 tbsp flour

About 500 ml / 2 cups milk

Salt and freshly ground pepper

Method

Prep and cook time: 1 h 20 min

1 Lightly grease an ovenproof dish with a little olive oil. Preheat the oven to 180C (350 F / Gas Mark 4).

2 Combine the garlic with the tomatoes. Season with salt and pepper.

3 Remove the basil leaves from the stems, chop the leaves and stir into the tomatoes.

4 Slice the mozzarella and reserve a few slices.

5 For the béchamel sauce, melt the butter in a pan, stir in the flour and cook briefly. Add the milk gradually while stirring. Simmer for about 10 minutes, stirring continuously. Season with salt and pepper.

6 Spoon a little of the béchamel sauce into the bottom of the baking dish.

7 Place a layer of lasagna sheets on top, then some of the tomato mixture and another layer of lasagna. Add some more béchamel sauce, some mozzarella and a few basil leaves.

8 Continue layering until all the ingredients have been used. Finish with béchamel sauce and the reserved mozzarella.

9 Sprinkle with the Parmesan cheese and season with salt and pepper.

10 Bake in the preheated oven for 40–45 minutes until golden brown.

SALTIMBOCCA SKEWERS

Ingredients

4 thin veal cutlets

4 slices prosciutto

24 sage leaves

1 lemon

2 handfuls arugula (rocket)

Pinch of sugar

3–4 tbsp olive oil

Salt and freshly ground pepper

Method
Prep and cook time: 1 h

1 Put the veal cutlets between two pieces of plastic wrap and pound lightly to flatten.

2 Lay the prosciutto on top of the cutlets and cut each cutlet lengthwise into three strips. Thread a cutlet strip with 2 sage leaves in a wave shape onto each skewer.

3 Rinse the lemon under hot water and rub dry. Slice in half. Squeeze the juice out of one half. Cut the other half into wedges.

4 Heat the broiler or grill.

5 Combine the lemon juice, a little salt and pepper, sugar and 3 tbsp of the olive oil to make a salad dressing.

6 Brush the skewers and the lemon pieces with some of the oil. Broil (grill) the meat for 1–2 minutes per side (the meat should be slightly pink inside). Grill the lemon pieces briefly until they start to color.

7 Season the meat with salt and pepper and drizzle with the rest of the olive oil. Toss the arugula (rocket) with the salad dressing and serve with the lemon pieces and kebabs.

FRITTATA WITH POTATO AND PEAS

Ingredients

675 g / 1½ lb waxy potatoes

20 g / 1 cup baby spinach leaves

6 eggs

3 tbsp whipping cream

Nutmeg

1 onion, sliced

2 tbsp olive oil

100 g / ⅔ cup frozen peas

1 tbsp chopped fresh basil

Salt and freshly ground pepper

Method

Prep and cook time: 45 min

1 Preheat the oven to 220C (425 F / Gas Mark 7).

2 Boil the potatoes in salted water for about 30 minutes or until they can be easily pierced with a knife. Allow to cool. Peel and cut into bite-size pieces.

3 Rinse and coarsely chop the spinach.

4 Whisk the eggs with the cream. Season with salt, pepper and nutmeg.

5 Sauté the onion slices in hot oil. Add the potatoes and continue to sauté until golden brown, about 2–3 minutes.

6 Add the peas, spinach and basil. Pour in the eggs. Cook briefly, then place in the preheated oven for about 8 minutes until set.

ASPARAGUS LASAGNA WITH SALMON AND TOMATOES

Ingredients

900 g / 2 lb white asparagus

¼ tsp sugar

4 ripe tomatoes

450 g / 1 lb salmon fillet, skinned

2 shallots

3 tbsp butter

2 tbsp flour

200 ml / scant cup milk

200 ml / scant cup whipping cream

Nutmeg

2 tbsp lemon Juice

225 g / ½ lb lasagna sheets, (no-precook type)

75 g / ¾ cup freshly grated Parmesan cheese

Salt and freshly ground pepper

Method

Prep and cook time: 1 h 30 min

1 Preheat the oven to 200C (400F / Gas Mark 6).

2 Peel the asparagus, cut off the ends and cook for about 8 minutes in salted water with the sugar.

3 Drain, catching the cooking liquor, refresh in cold water and drain thoroughly. Set the cooking liquor aside.

4 Drop the tomatoes into boiling water for a few seconds, then skin, quarter, deseed and dice.

5 Slice the salmon across into about 1 cm / ¼ inch slices.

6 Peel and finely dice the shallots. Heat 2 tbsp butter in a pan and sweat the shallots until translucent.

7 Sprinkle with the flour and cook for a couple of minutes without browning, then stir in the milk and cream.

8 Bring to a boil, stirring until smooth. Add approximately 1⅔ cups of the asparagus cooking liquor, season with salt, pepper, nutmeg and lemon juice, and simmer for a few minutes.

9 Grease an ovenproof dish with the rest of the butter.

10 Cover the base with sheets of lasagna, and add a layer of asparagus and tomatoes, then a layer of sauce. Place another layer of lasagna on top of the sauce, then add a layer of salmon and more sauce. Repeat the process but finish off with a layer of asparagus and tomatoes.

11 Pour the rest of the sauce over and sprinkle with Parmesan cheese. Bake in the preheated oven for about 40 minutes.

SALMON WITH MOZZARELLA, TOMATOES AND BASIL

Ingredients

For the salad:

400 g / 2 cups mozzarella cheese

4 tomatoes

1 tbsp pumpkin seed oil

1 tbsp olive oil

3 tbsp white balsamic vinegar

Salt and freshly ground pepper

For the fish:

1 slice melba toast

30 g / 1 cup basil leaves

2 tbsp pine nuts

2 tbsp freshly grated Parmesan cheese

1 egg yolk

About 4 tbsp olive oil

675 g / 1½ lb salmon fillet

Salt and freshly ground pepper

Basil, for garnishing

Method

Prep and cook time: 40 min

1 Slice the mozzarella into 8 pieces. Divide among four deep plates.

2 Rinse the tomatoes, cut out the cores and slice. Decorate each plate with tomato slices. Season lightly with salt and pepper.

3 Mix the oils with the balsamic vinegar. Drizzle over the salad and allow to marinate.

4 Remove the crust from the melba toast. Break the bread into crumbs.

5 Put the bread crumbs, basil leaves, pine nuts, Parmesan cheese, egg yolk and about 2 tbsp of olive oil in a food processor. Purée into a paste.

6 Rinse the salmon and pat dry. Slice into 4 pieces.

7 Slice a little pocket into the sides of each piece of fish with a knife and fill with the paste.

8 Gently sauté the fish in hot oil for 3–4 minutes on each side, until golden brown. Season with salt and pepper. Cut in half and arrange on top of the salad. Garnish with the fresh basil and serve.

RAVIOLI WITH SPINACH AND SAGE

Ingredients

450 g / 1 lb all-purpose (plain) flour

4 eggs

5 tbsp dry white wine

150 g / 6 oz spinach

3 tbsp bread crumbs

200 g / 2 cups ricotta cheese

2 tbsp freshly grated Parmesan cheese, plus extra to serve

2 tsp lemon juice

4 tbsp butter

10 g / ½ cup small sage leaves

Salt and freshly ground pepper

Method

Prep and cook time: 50 min plus 30 min resting time

1 Mix the flour, 3 eggs, the wine and a little salt to form a smooth dough. Shape the dough into a ball and wrap in plastic wrap. Allow to rest for at least 30 minutes.

2 Rinse the spinach well. Discard any discolored or ragged leaves. Wilt the slightly wet spinach in a pan over a medium heat. Place in a colander, refresh under cold water and drain well. Squeeze out as much water as possible. Finely chop.

3 Mix the bread crumbs, ricotta, the remaining egg and the Parmesan cheese in a bowl.

4 Mix in the spinach and season with the lemon juice, salt and pepper.

5 Roll out the pasta dough with a pasta machine or with a rolling pin on a floured work surface to about ¼ cm / $^1/_{16}$ inch thick. Cut into 5 cm / 2 inch wide strips.

6 Place teaspoons of filling 5 cm / 2 inches apart on one strip of pasta, moisten the edges and in between each piece of filling, and cover with a second strip.

7 Seal the dough around the filling and cut the ravioli into squares with a pastry wheel.

8 Melt the butter with a few sage leaves.

9 Put a large pan of salted water on to boil. Cook the ravioli in batches by dropping into the boiling water. Immediately lower the heat. Simmer for 3–5 minutes. Remove from the pan and drain well.

10 Arrange the ravioli on plates. Pour the melted sage butter over the top. Sprinkle with the Parmesan. Serve.

POTATO AND TOMATO SALAD WITH PESTO DRESSING

Ingredients

900 g / 2 lb small, new potatoes

675 g / 1½ lb small tomatoes

For the pesto:

4 sprigs fresh basil

2 sprigs fresh parsley

2 garlic cloves

50 g / ½ cup pine nuts

50 g / ½ cup Parmesan cheese

About 7 tbsp olive oil

3 tbsp lemon juice

Salt and freshly ground pepper

8 slices prosciutto, to serve

Method

Prep and cook time: 40 min

1 Boil the potatoes in well-salted water for about 25 minutes until you can pierce them easily with a fork.

2 Cut the tomatoes in half.

3 Remove the basil and parsley leaves from the stems. Put the herbs along with the peeled garlic, pine nuts and Parmesan into a food processor. Chop coarsely. Gradually add enough olive oil to make a thin paste. Season with the lemon juice, salt and pepper.

4 Drain the potatoes and allow some of the excess water to evaporate. Slice in half and gently mix with the tomatoes and pesto dressing.

5 Arrange on plates with the prosciutto and serve.

LAMB CHOPS
WITH PESTO

Ingredients

40 g / 2 cups basil leaves

2 garlic cloves, peeled

1 tbsp pine nuts

Olive oil

2 handfuls arugula (rocket)

8 lamb chops

Salt and freshly ground pepper

Method

Prep and cook time: 25 min

1 For the pesto, pick off the basil leaves and purée with the peeled garlic, pine nuts and sufficient oil to produce a creamy mixture, adding the oil in a steady stream. Season to taste with salt and pepper.

2 Arrange the arugula (rocket) on plates.

3 Wash and dry the chops and season with salt and pepper.

4 Heat a little oil and fry the chops for 2–3 minutes on each side, or until golden brown.

5 Place two lamb chops on each plate and serve drizzled with pesto.

SAFFRON PASTA
WITH SPRING VEGETABLES

Ingredients

For the saffron pasta:

8 threads saffron

300 g / 3 cups all-purpose
(plain) flour

1 tsp salt

4 egg yolks

2 whole eggs

For the vegetables:

225 g / ½ lb broccoli

½ small zucchini (courgette)

100 g / ¼ lb snow peas (sugar snaps)

225 g / ½ lb green asparagus

2 tbsp olive oil

3 tbsp vegetable broth (stock)

Chives

Salt and freshly ground pepper

Freshly grated Parmesan cheese,
to serve

Method

Prep and cook time: 45 min plus 30 min resting time

1 Infuse the saffron threads in 1 tbsp hot water.

2 Put the flour and salt in a heap on a work surface, make a well in the center and add the egg yolks, eggs and saffron liquid.

3 Whisk the eggs into the flour with a fork, adding a little water if necessary, and knead to a smooth, glossy dough. Form the dough into a ball, wrap in plastic wrap (cling film) and leave to rest for at least 30 minutes.

4 Prepare the vegetables: divide the broccoli into florets and peel the stalk. Dice the zucchini (courgette). Peel the lower third of the asparagus spears and cut each into 3. Wash the snow peas (sugar snaps).

5 Bring some salted water to a boil and blanch the vegetables in batches for 3 to 4 minutes. Drain each batch, refresh in iced water and drain thoroughly.

6 Roll out the dough thinly, either by hand or in a pasta machine, and cut into strips. Cook in plenty of boiling, salted water until al dente. Drain well.

7 Heat the oil in a wok or a deep skillet until it foams, add the vegetables and stir.

8 Add the vegetable broth (stock), season with salt and pepper and cook for 3 minutes.

9 Add the drained saffron pasta and mix well.

10 Trim the chives and scatter over the pasta and vegetables. Serve with Parmesan cheese.

PEPERONATA

Ingredients

350 g / ¾ lb tomatoes

6 tbsp olive oil

3 scallions (spring onions), sliced

2 garlic cloves, chopped

450 g / 1 lb red bell peppers, halved and deseeded

450 g / 1 lb yellow bell peppers, halved and deseeded

450 g / 1 lb green bell peppers, halved and deseeded

2 tsp dried oregano

50 g / ½ cup black olives

Basil, to garnish

Salt and freshly ground pepper

Method

Prep and cook time: 40 min plus at least 1h to marinate

1 Preheat the oven to 240C (475F / Gas Mark 9).

2 Roughly chop the tomatoes, put them in a covered dish with 2 tbsp of the olive oil and 1 tsp salt and allow to marinate for about 30 minutes.

3 Heat 2 tbsp olive oil in a pan and gently cook the scallions (spring onions) and garlic until softened.

4 Place the halved bell peppers on an oven rack on a roasting pan and roast in the oven for 10–15 minutes. Cover with a damp kitchen towel. Allow to cool slightly and then remove the skins.

5 Coarsely chop the bell peppers and mix them with the scallions.

6 Blend the tomatoes with a hand blender and pass though a sieve to remove seeds and skins. Season with salt and pepper.

7 Mix the skinned bell peppers and scallions with the tomato sauce and stir in the oregano. Allow to sit for at least 30 minutes and season with salt and pepper.

8 To serve, sprinkle the olives on top and garnish with basil.

RIBBON NOODLES WITH LAMB RAGOUT

Ingredients

3 tbsp olive oil

900 g / 2 lb lamb, cut into bite-size pieces

2 onions, chopped

2 garlic cloves, chopped

1 tbsp tomato paste (purée)

100 ml / 7 tbsp dry red wine

250 ml / 1 cup beef broth (stock)

400 g / 2 cups canned tomatoes, chopped

1 sprig rosemary

1 bay leaf

450 g / 1 lb pappardelle

Salt and freshly ground pepper

Fresh rosemary, for garnishing

Method

Prep and cook time: 1 h 20 min

1 Heat the oil in a large pan and sear the meat until brown all over

2 Add the onions, garlic and tomato paste (purée) and continue to fry for 2 minutes more.

3 Pour in the red wine. Simmer briefly.

4 Add the broth (stock) and the tomatoes, bring to a boil and season with salt and pepper.

5 Add the sprig of rosemary and the bay leaf to the sauce. Simmer gently for about 1 hour, stirring occasionally. Add a little water to the sauce if needed.

6 Cook the noodles in well-salted boiling water until al dente.

7 Remove the rosemary and the bay leaf from the ragout. Season to taste with salt and pepper.

8 Drain the pasta and divide among 4 plates. Pour the ragout over the top and garnish with the fresh rosemary.

PENNE
WITH WHITE BEANS AND PESTO

Ingredients

450 g / 1 lb penne

250 g / 1¼ cups canned white beans

20 g / 1 cup fresh basil leaves

20 g / 1 cup arugula (rocket)

1 sprig parsley

1 garlic clove

50 g / ½ cup pine nuts

About 3 tbsp olive oil

1 lemon

25 g / ¼ cup Parmesan cheese

Salt and freshly ground pepper

Method

Prep and cook time: 20 min

1 Boil the penne in salted water until al dente.

2 Put the beans in a sieve. Rinse and drain.

3 Rinse the basil, arugula (rocket) and parsley leaves and shake dry. Discard any discolored leaves. Put all the leaves in a food processor.

4 Peel the garlic clove and add it to the herbs along with the pine nuts. Pour in the olive oil and 1–2 tbsp of the penne cooking water. Purée until smooth.

5 Remove the zest from the lemon. Squeeze out the juice. Season the pesto with the lemon juice, salt and pepper.

6 Put the beans in with the penne during the last 2 minutes of cooking time. Drain.

7 Combine the pesto with the beans and penne. Divide among the plates. Sprinkle with the lemon zest and Parmesan cheese. Serve.

FRIED MOZZARELLA WITH TOMATO SALSA

Ingredients

For the mozzarella balls:

4 mozzarella balls, approx.
150 g / 6 oz each

2 tbsp all-purpose (plain) flour

1 egg, well beaten

50 g / ½ cup bread crumbs

Oil, for frying

Basil, for garnishing

Salt and freshly ground pepper

For the salsa:

4 tomatoes

1 red chili pepper, deseeded and
finely chopped

1 red onion, chopped

1 tbsp cilantro (fresh coriander) leaves,
chopped

2 tbsp olive oil

Lemon juice

Sugar

Sea salt

Pesto from a jar, to serve

Method

Prep and cook time: 45 min

1 For the salsa plunge the tomatoes in boiling water for 30 seconds, discard the skin and seeds and chop the flesh.

2 Mix the chili, onion and cilantro (fresh coriander) leaves with the olive oil. Season to taste with the lemon juice, sugar and sea salt.

3 Drain the mozzarella balls well. Dredge them with seasoned flour. Dip in the beaten egg and dredge with the bread crumbs. Fry in hot oil (170C / 325F) until golden brown.

4 Place a fried mozzarella ball on each. Garnish with pesto and fresh basil and serve with the salsa.

SARDINES WITH TOMATO AND EGG VINAIGRETTE

Ingredients

24 fresh sardines (ready to cook, deboned, heads removed)

Flour, for dredging

8 tbsp olive oil

3 tomatoes

2 eggs

3 tbsp balsamic vinegar

2½ tsp sugar

1 radicchio lettuce

Salt and freshly ground pepper

Fresh basil leaves, to garnish

Method

Prep and cook time: 30 min

1 Rinse the sardines well under cold water. Pat dry.

2 Dredge the sardines in the flour. Sauté on both sides in 2 tbsp of hot oil for about 3 minutes until golden brown. Season with salt and pepper. Remove from the pan. Allow to drain on paper towels.

3 Blanch the tomatoes for a few seconds. Refresh in cold water. Remove the skins and cut into quarters. Remove the seeds and finely chop.

4 Hard boil the eggs. Refresh in cold water. Peel and chop. Mix with the balsamic vinegar and the remaining olive oil. Add the tomatoes. Season with salt, pepper and sugar.

5 Remove the core from the radicchio. Slice into 1 cm / ½ inch wide pieces.

6 Divide the radicchio and sardines among the plates. Pour the tomato and egg vinaigrette over the top. Garnish with the basil. Serve lukewarm or cold.

WATERMELON GRANITA

Ingredients

100 g / ½ cup sugar

450 g / 1 lb watermelon flesh

Juice of 1 lemon

1 tsp rosewater

Method

Prep and cook time: 15 min plus 4 h freezer time

1 Put the sugar in a pan with 100 ml / ½ cup of water and bring to a boil. Boil for about 1 minute. Remove from the heat and allow to cool.

2 Finely chop the watermelon. Purée with in a blender.

3 Combine the syrup, lemon juice and rosewater. Add to the watermelon purée. Place the mixture in a flat metal container. Freeze for at least 4 hours, stirring well with a fork every half hour for the first 3 hours.

4 Fill small bowls with the granita and serve.

TORTA DELLA NONNA

Ingredients

For the dough:

300 g / 3 cups flour

1 egg yolk

1 egg

200 g / 1 cup butter, flaked

100 g / ²/₃ cup ground almonds

2½ tsp salt

50 g / ¼ cup sugar

For the filling:

400 ml / 1²/₃ cups milk

1 tsp vanilla extract

4 egg yolks

50 g / ¼ cup sugar

2 tbsp corn starch (cornflour), mixed with a little water

½ tsp lemon zest

50 g / ½ cup pine nuts

Confectioners' (icing) sugar, for dusting

Method

Prep and cook time: 1 h plus 30 min resting time

1 Mound the flour on a work surface. Make a well in the middle and put in the egg yolk, egg and flaked butter.

2 Add the almonds, salt and sugar. Working from the middle, knead into a smooth dough. Wrap in plastic wrap and chill for about 30 minutes.

3 To make the filling, bring the milk and the vanilla extract to a boil while stirring. Stir in the egg yolk, sugar and lemon zest and add the corn starch (cornflour). Cook while stirring continuously until creamy.

4 Pour the cream through a sieve into a bowl and allow to cool to room temperature.

5 Preheat the oven to 180C (350 F / Gas Mark 4).

6 Roll out the dough. Use it to line a 26 cm / 10 inch springform pan, the dough coming 3 cm / 1½ inches above the top of the pan. Prick the crust all over with a fork.

7 Pour the filling over the crust and smooth. Sprinkle with the pine nuts and fold the edges of the dough over the filling.

8 Bake in the preheated oven for about 40 minutes until golden brown. Allow to cool slightly then remove the sides of the pan. Cool to room temperature on a wire rack. Dust with confectioners' (icing) sugar and serve.

CAFFÈ LATTE
ICE CREAM

Ingredients

2 eggs

70 g / ⅓ cup sugar

150 ml / ⅔ cup milk

150 ml / ⅔ cup espresso

200 ml / scant cup whipping cream

100 g / 1 cup chopped dark chocolate, 70% cocoa solids

To decorate:

100 ml / 7 tbsp milk

Mint leaves

1 cup raspberries

Method

Prep and cook time: 25 min plus 4h freezing time

1 Whisk together the eggs, sugar, milk and espresso in a large bowl set over a pan of simmering water until the mixture is thick and creamy.

2 Let the mixture cool, stirring from time to time.

3 Whip the cream until stiff peaks form. Fold the cream and chocolate into the cold egg mixture.

4 Put the mixture to churn in an ice cream machine, or pour into a flat metal dish and freeze for at least 4 hours, stirring well every 30 minutes.

5 To serve, use a scoop to put the ice cream into dessert glasses. Pour chilled milk over the top, garnish with mint and decorate with the raspberries.

PANNA COTTA
WITH RASPBERRIES

Ingredients

1 vanilla bean

500 ml / 2 cups whipping cream

50 g / ¼ cup sugar

3 leaves white gelatin

½ tsp lemon zest

225 g / ½ lb raspberries

Method

Prep and cook time: 15 min plus at least
5 h chilling time

1 Slice the vanilla bean in half lengthwise. Scrape out the seeds.

2 Cook the cream with the sugar, vanilla seeds and pod over low heat for about 3 minutes.

3 Soften the gelatin in a dish with cold water.

4 Remove the vanilla bean from the cream. Remove the pan from the heat.

5 Squeeze out the gelatin and add it to the vanilla cream. Stir to dissolve. Add the lemon zest.

6 Rinse out 4 molds with cold water. Fill with the cream and refrigerate for at least 5 hours.

7 Turn the panna cotta out of the molds (to dislodge: briefly dip the molds in hot water). Decorate with the raspberries and serve.

TIRAMISÙ

Ingredients

5 egg yolks

50 g / ½ cup confectioners' (icing) sugar

500 g / 2 cups mascarpone

3 tbsp almond liqueur

500 ml / 2 cups strong espresso

16 lady fingers (sponge fingers)

Cocoa powder, for dusting

Confectioners' (icing) sugar, for dusting

Method

Prep and cook time: 30 min

1 Beat the egg yolks and confectioners' (icing) sugar until foaming, then stir in the mascarpone and the liqueur.

2 Put the espresso in a flat dish, dip half of the sponge fingers in the espresso and lay them on the base of a rectangular serving dish.

3 Spread with half of the egg/cream mixture and dust with cocoa. Repeat the process with the remaining sponge fingers and mascarpone cream. Dust with cocoa and confectioners' sugar before serving.

CHILLED RICOTTA WITH CANDIED FRUIT

Ingredients

150 g / 2 cups mixed candied fruit

300 g / 1½ cups ricotta cheese

40 ml maraschino liqueur

50 g / ½ cup confectioners' (icing) sugar

1 lemon, zest and juice

250 ml / 1 cup whipping cream

To decorate:

Blackcurrants

Mint leaves

Confectioners' (icing) sugar, for dusting

Method

Prep and cook time: 20 min plus 4 h freezing time

1 Chop the candied fruit.

2 Mix together the ricotta, maraschino, sugar, lemon juice and zest until smooth.

3 Whip the cream until stiff peaks form. Mix together the cream, fruit and ricotta mixture.

4 Line 4 molds, each 250 ml / 1 cup capacity, with plastic wrap. Divide the mixture between the molds and freeze for at least 4 hours.

5 About 10 minutes before serving, remove the molds from the freezer. Turn them out onto four plates (to dislodge: dip the molds briefly in hot water). Decorate with the blackcurrants and mint. Dust with the confectioners' (icing) sugar.

ZUCCOTTO

Ingredients

For the sponge cake:

5 eggs

100 g / 1 cup confectioners' (icing) sugar

50 g / ½ cup flour

50 g / ½ cup corn starch (cornflour)

2 tbsp sugar, for the kitchen towel

3 tbsp amaretto, for soaking

For the filling:

150 g / 1½ cups chopped dark chocolate, 60% cocoa solids

500 ml / 2 cups whipping cream

75 g / ¾ cup confectioners' (icing) sugar

300 g / 1½ cups ricotta cheese

1 tsp vanilla extract

100 g / ½ cup mixed chopped candied fruit

Cocoa powder, for dusting

Confectioners' (icing) sugar, for dusting

Method

Prep and cook time: 1 h 30 min
plus about 4 hrs chilling time

1 Line a large cookie sheet with parchment paper. Preheat the oven to 180C (350F / Gas Mark 4).

2 Separate the eggs. Whip the egg yolks with the sugar until very foamy.

3 Whip the eggs whites until stiff peaks form. Fold into the egg yolks.

4 Sift the flour and corn starch (cornflour) into the egg mixture. Carefully fold in.

5 Spread the mixture evenly onto the cookie sheet and bake in the preheated oven for about 15 minutes.

6 Turn the cake out onto a kitchen towel which has been dusted with the sugar. Gently remove the paper. Allow to cool completely.

7 Line a cake dome or large bowl (2 liter / 2 quart capacity) with plastic wrap. Cut the sponge cake into triangular wedges. Use some of the triangles to line the dome to the rim. Brush with the amaretto.

8 Melt the chocolate with 4 tbsp of cream over a hot water bath. Put aside and allow to cool slightly.

9 Whip the remaining cream with ½ cup (50 g) of the confectioners' (icing) sugar.

10 Combine the ricotta, vanilla extract and remaining sugar. Fold into the cream.

11 Take one third of the cream/ricotta mixture, and mix it carefully with the cooled (but still melted) chocolate. Mix the remaining cream/ricotta with the candied fruit.

12 Spoon the fruit mixture into the form and smooth the surface. Place a layer of sponge cake on top. Chill for 20 minutes.

13 Place the chocolate cream on top. Cover with the remaining sponge cake. Chill for at least 3 hours.

14 Before serving, turn the cake out onto a platter. Remove the plastic wrap. Refrigerate for 30 minutes. Dust with the cocoa powder and confectioners' sugar. Slice and serve.

Published by Transatlantic Press

First published in 2010

Transatlantic Press
38 Copthorne Road, Croxley Green, Hertfordshire WD3 4AQ

© Transatlantic Press

Images and Recipes by StockFood © The Food Image Agency

Recipes selected by Marika Kucerova, StockFood

A catalogue record for this book is available from the British Library.

ISBN: 978–1–907176–46–3

Printed in China